D0365354

COUNT ON ME
Sports

Remarkable Stories of
TEAMWORK
in sports

BRAD HERZOG

"As shown by the wonderful stories in Count on Me: Sports, athletics can not only reveal character, but also inspire it."
—**Shannon Miller,** two-time Olympic gold medalist in gymnastics

"The true tales in Brad Herzog's books show how the games we play can teach seriously important life lessons."
—**Jake Delhomme,** former Super Bowl quarterback for the Carolina Panthers

free spirit
PUBLISHING®

Library of Congress Cataloging-in-Publication Data
Herzog, Brad.
  Remarkable stories of teamwork in sports / by Brad Herzog.
    pages cm. — (Count on me: Sports)
  Includes bibliographical references and index.
  Audience: Age: 8–13.
  ISBN 978-1-57542-479-8 — ISBN 1-57542-479-7 1. Teamwork (Sports)—Juvenile literature. I. Title.
  GV706.8.H47 2014
  796—dc23
                                                                    2014004698

Reading Level Grade 5; Interest Level Ages 8–13;
Fountas & Pinnell Guided Reading Level V

Edited by Alison Behnke
Cover and interior design by Michelle Lee Lagerroos

Cover photo credits: background © Bruxov | Dreamstime.com; clockwise from top left: AP Photo/Rob Stapleton; AP Photo/Lisa Poole; AP Photo/Julie Oliver, Ottawa Citizen; AP Photo/Mark J. Terrill; Bettmann/Corbis/AP Images; AP Photo/Jim Mone. For interior photo credits, see page 102.

10 9 8 7 6 5 4 3 2 1
Printed in the United States of America
S18860614

Free Spirit Publishing Inc.
Minneapolis, MN
(612) 338-2068
help4kids@freespirit.com
www.freespirit.com

DEDICATION

For the Taorminas (Michael, Romy, Coleman, and Nathan) and the Marshalls (Greg, Dana, Connor, Cameron, and Ava). We all make a good team.

ACKNOWLEDGMENTS

Thank you to Judy Galbraith, Margie Lisovskis, and the rest of the crew at Free Spirit Publishing for having the courage to pursue a series of books celebrating stories of character in sports. I found Alison Behnke to be both insightful and inclusive as an editor, an author's dream combination, and Michelle Lee Lagerroos put in overtime making sure the designs were just right. Finally, I am grateful to Aimee Jackson for bringing me to Free Spirit in the first place and for her unwavering support and friendship.

CONTENTS

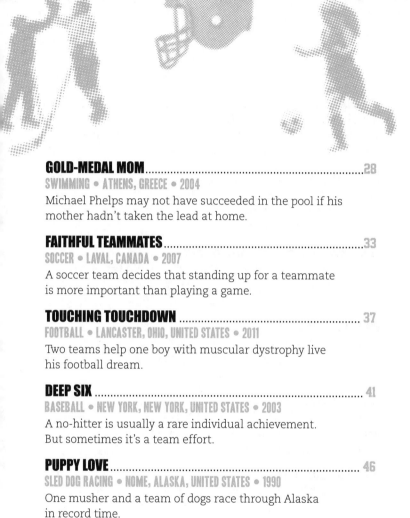

INTRODUCTION

At the 1980 Winter Olympics in Lake Placid, New York, the odds were stacked against the U.S. hockey team. Most people figured they had no chance of winning. But then they surprised everyone by winning four games.

Still, even as the U.S. players moved on to the first medal round, most people didn't think they could win. After all, their next opponent was a team from the Soviet Union. (The Soviet Union split apart in 1991. The former Soviet Union is now many countries, including Russia and Ukraine.) The Soviets had dominated Olympic ice hockey for decades. A year earlier, they had defeated a team of National Hockey League all-stars in a 6–0 rout. Meanwhile, the U.S. squad was a bunch of unknown college and minor league players. Some would go on to have great professional careers. But at the time, they were young and inexperienced. In an exhibition game before the Olympics, the Soviets beat the Americans 10–3.

Yet something magical happened that February in Lake Placid. It was one of the most stunning upsets in sports history. In the third period, U.S. team captain Mike Eruzione scored a goal. That put the Americans ahead 4–3. For the last 10 minutes, the U.S. players managed to keep the Soviets from scoring. The crowd cheered wildly the whole time. "Do you believe in miracles?" TV sportscaster Al Michaels famously asked, as the clock ticked down to zero. "Yes!" The fans went wild.

The U.S. team went on to defeat Finland in the final game. With that victory, they stunned the world and took home a gold medal.

The moment will forever be known as the "Miracle on Ice." But was it a *miracle?* Or was it a great example of preparation and teamwork? Before his team took on the Soviets, U.S. coach Herb Brooks had talked to the players honestly. "Gentlemen," he said, "you don't have enough talent to win on talent alone."

But teamwork was even more important than talent. That's what this book is all about.

This is a collection of tales about what it means to be a good teammate, in every sense of the word. Some people in this book will inspire you, like the Brooklyn Dodger who stood by a teammate when few others did, and the girls' softball team that traded an easy victory for a chance to aid a rival team. Some performances will amaze you, like the father who helped his paralyzed son be an endurance racing legend, and the 10-year-old caddie who played a central role in golf's greatest upset.

Teamwork can show up in many different ways. Teammates can overcome obstacles or light up someone's life. They can support a struggling friend or stranger. They can even achieve something that seems impossible. Many people have said that the letters in TEAM could stand for Together Everyone Achieves More. The stories in these pages certainly prove that.

And all these stories share one simple fact—one secret to success. Pat Summitt, a Hall of Fame women's basketball coach, knows the secret well. She discovered it on her way to more than 1,000 victories and eight national championships: "Teamwork is what makes common people capable of uncommon results."

TEAM HOYT

APRIL 15, 2013 • BOSTON, MASSACHUSETTS, UNITED STATES

Nobody will ever forget the 2013 Boston Marathon. About two hours after the winner finished the race, two bombs exploded. A pair of brothers had terrorized the city by planting these bombs near the finish line. The explosions killed 3 people and injured 264 others. Officials stopped the marathon right away. Thousands of runners were not able to finish the race. These racers included a father and son duo named Dick and Rick Hoyt. They had to stop about a mile short of the finish line.

The Hoyts had started the race not far from a statue of themselves. This statue had been unveiled a week earlier. It stands in front of an elementary school. This school is a place where many athletes in wheelchairs gather before each year's marathon. Dick and Rick Hoyt are an inspiration to all of them.

When Rick Hoyt was born in 1962, doctors talked to his parents right away. The doctors told them all about what their son couldn't do. The umbilical cord had gotten twisted around his neck, cutting off oxygen flow. Rick was born with cerebral palsy. He would never walk or speak.

But Rick went on to graduate from Boston University with a degree in special education. And the 2013 Boston Marathon marked the 31st time Rick had participated in the famous race. He hasn't done it alone, however. His dad has been with him every step of the way.

It was a long road to becoming a racing legend. Some medical experts said Rick should live in a special institution where nurses would care for him. But his parents, Dick and Judy, wanted their son with them.

When Rick was a child, his parents saw how his eyes followed them around the room. They noticed how he laughed at jokes. They realized he was smart. Slowly, patiently, they taught him the alphabet. They wanted to make sure there were no limits on what he could do.

When Rick was 11, he got a special computer. Using it, he could type by touching a switch with the side of his head. At the time, the Boston Bruins—his hometown hockey team—were trying to win the NHL's Stanley Cup. Rick's first words were, "Go Bruins!"

Not only was Rick bright, he was also a big sports fan. So one day in 1977, he asked his father if it would be possible to compete in a running race. How could his dad say no?

Dick Hoyt was not a runner at the time. But he pushed his son in a wheelchair for five kilometers.

MARATHON MEN

Jonathan Brunot was born with severe autism. He can only say and understand a handful of words. But three of them are *run*, *race*, and *marathon*.

At one time, Brunot had refused to run at all. But then Vincent Del-Cid talked to Brunot's mother. Del-Cid had run nearly two dozen marathons. He was also a volunteer for the Rolling Thunder Special Needs Program. He told Brunot's mother, "If you allow me to, I'll help him run a marathon." His mother wasn't sure at first. But in November 2008, at 19 years old, Brunot completed the New York City Marathon. He didn't stop there. In April 2012, he completed his fourth Boston Marathon. Now another word in Brunot's vocabulary is *Vincent*.

Afterward, Rick typed a message. He said, "Dad, when we were running, it felt like I wasn't disabled anymore."

The ultimate team was born.

While Rick was at school or studying, Dick began practicing. Every day he ran behind a wheelchair. He loaded the wheelchair with a bag of cement. He imagined racing with his son as Team Hoyt. With this idea as his inspiration, he worked hard and got into excellent shape. Father and son have competed in more than 1,000 endurance races. The list includes more than 70 marathons. Team Hoyt's best marathon time was in 1992. They completed that race in just under 2 hours and 41 minutes. That's only about 37 minutes slower than the marathon world record for men!

Team Hoyt also completed nearly 250 triathlons. These three-part races are made up of swimming, cycling, and running. For the swimming portion,

Dick attached a rope to his body and pulled Rick in a small boat. During the cycling part of the race, Rick rode on the front of a specially designed bike.

Over the years, Dick has carried his son up mountains. He pulled him on skis across snow-covered terrain. In 1992, he even biked and ran with him all the way across America. It was a trip of 3,735 miles. Team Hoyt did it in just 45 days.

Father and son raced on and on. Naturally, as Rick turned 50 and Dick turned 70, they slowed down a bit. That only meant they were running two dozen races a year instead of four dozen.

Rick describes Dick as the "Father of the Century." He only wishes he could repay him for all the years of dedication and support. "The thing I'd most like," he told a reporter, "is for my dad to sit in the chair, and I would push him for once."

The 2013 Boston Marathon bombings were a reminder that bad people exist in the world. Sometimes terrible tragedies happen. But people like the Hoyts remind us that the world has very good people, too. Just like a marathon is a test of endurance, teamwork and kindness can also endure.

NEVER FORGOTTEN

MARCH 3, 2011 • FENNVILLE, MICHIGAN, UNITED STATES

On March 3, 2011, basketball star Wes Leonard scored a game-winning layup. He led his Fennville High Blackhawks to a 57–55 victory in overtime. It was a big win. It clinched an undefeated regular season.

The performance was typical of Leonard. At 16, he was the best player on the team. And he was great under pressure. But that wasn't all. He was heroic in many ways. He was the kind of guy who sank winning baskets, tossed no-hitters, and threw touchdown passes. He was also the kind of guy who befriended a classmate with autism and sat with her during lunch. It was easy to love Wes Leonard.

When the buzzer sounded after Leonard's layup, his teammates hoisted him into the air. He shook hands with the other team. Then, as he started walking off the court, his knees buckled. Leonard collapsed. Joy and pride turned to fear. Leonard was having a heart attack. Nearby, the school had a machine that could have shocked his heart back into rhythm. But the battery was dead. Though paramedics worked frantically to save Leonard, he died at the hospital two hours later.

What does a community do after such a tragedy? In Fennville, they came together. Leonard's teammates, coaches, and even people who had never met him rallied around his memory.

Some of Leonard's teammates slept at the family's house for a week. They spent a lot of time with Wes's 13-year-old brother Mitchell. Eventually, Mitchell took a place on the Blackhawks bench.

Other basketball players also stepped up after Leonard's death. Former NBA player Bo Kimble came and spoke to the team. One of Kimble's own teammates had died of heart failure 21 years earlier. Tom

Izzo, the coach of the Michigan State basketball team, also talked to the Blackhawks and gave his support.

In addition, Wes's mom and dad, Gary and Jocelyn, got letters from parents all over the country. These parents had also lost their young athlete sons—a wrestler in Oregon, a football player in Nebraska, a

A HAND FOR HANK

In 1990, Loyola Marymount University's basketball team was playing in the semifinals of the West Coast Conference Tournament. Suddenly, Loyola star Eric "Hank" Gathers collapsed and died from a heart problem. Players, coaches, and fans reeled from the tragedy. Officials called off the event. The league also decided to let Loyola automatically move on to the NCAA Tournament.

Bo Kimble was the team's other big star. Kimble was right-handed. But in memory of Gathers, Kimble pledged to shoot the first free throw of every tournament game left-handed. Gathers had often done that as a way to improve his shooting. So Kimble did the same. His first shot was good. *Swish.* The team made it to the next round . . . *swish.* And the Sweet Sixteen . . . *swish.* And the Elite Eight . . . *swish!* It was a perfect tribute to a teammate.

basketball player in Georgia—to heart problems. None of these people ever met Leonard. But they became part of the team in honoring his memory.

Leonard's parents said that he would have wanted the Blackhawks to continue their season in the play-offs. When Fennville took the court again, Gary and Jocelyn were there. Through tears, they supported their son's team. They watched as the Fennville players walked on the court arm in arm, led by Wes's brother. They saw that both the Blackhawks and the opposing team warmed up in jerseys that said LEONARD and #35 (his number). They cheered for Leonard's best friend, Xavier Grigg. Grigg had replaced Leonard in the starting lineup and scored 11 fourth-quarter points. In Leonard's place, Grigg led the team to a playoff victory.

Even without their fallen star, Fennville won the next game, too. A few days later they played in the district championship game. They pulled off a come-from-behind 51–48 victory over Covert High. At the game's end, Mitchell Leonard took the court. Wearing a T-shirt adorned with the words "NEVER FORGOTTEN," he lifted the championship trophy above his head. "They are like brothers to me now," he said about his new teammates. "They always will be. They are like family."

DODGING NOTHING

1947 • CINCINNATI, OHIO, UNITED STATES

In autumn 2005, a minor league ballpark in Brooklyn, New York, unveiled a statue. It shows two baseball players, Jackie Robinson and Harold "Pee Wee" Reese. Neither of them is in action. One simply has his arm around the shoulder of the other. But the statue just might show the greatest play in baseball history.

In 1947, Pee Wee Reese was the star shortstop for the Brooklyn Dodgers. His team was about to make history. As a new member of the Dodgers, Jackie Robinson broke baseball's racial barrier. He was the first black player in the major leagues. But some of his teammates were racist. They wanted their team to stay all white. So they passed around a petition announcing they would refuse to play with Robinson. Reese—one of the team's most respected members— refused to sign it.

As the season began, Robinson faced many challenges on and off the field. For example, a Philadelphia hotel would not let him stay there. At games, some opposing players pointed bats at him and made machine gun noises. As time went on, the pressure on Robinson hurt his game. He went hitless in 20 straight at bats. One sports writer described him as "the loneliest man I have ever seen in sports."

So why the statue? Because one day, Reese made a simple move. With one gesture, he told the world: *This is my teammate.*

The facts surrounding the moment are hazy after all these years. But its impact was powerful. As Robinson stood next to first base, the crowd at old Crosley Field in Cincinnati, Ohio, shouted at him. Some said terrible, hateful things about Robinson and the color of his skin. Listening from his shortstop position, Reese got more and more angry. "Something in my gut reacted at the moment," he explained years later. "Something about what? The unfairness of it? The injustice of it? I don't know."

So he walked across the infield to Robinson. With his presence, he sent a small but important message of support. In his autobiography, Robinson said, "Pee Wee kind of sensed the sort of helpless, dead feeling in me and came over and stood beside me for a while.

He didn't say a word, but he looked over at the chaps who were yelling at me and just stared." The heckling stopped. "He was standing by me, I could tell you that," Robinson wrote. "I will never forget it."

Robinson's wife, Rachel, didn't forget either. The day the statue was unveiled, she talked about that moment. "I remember Jackie talking about Pee Wee's gesture the day it happened," she said. "It came as such a relief to him that a teammate and the captain of the team would go out of his way in such a public fashion to express friendship."

The Dodgers went on to win the National League pennant. Robinson was named Rookie of the Year. Two years later, he was named the league's Most Valuable Player. Today, he is a member of the

National Baseball Hall of Fame. So is his old team-mate, a guy nicknamed "Pee Wee" who came up big when it counted.

Later, Reese shrugged off the moment as simply the right thing to do. But his son, Mark, knew how important it was. "My father had done his own soul searching. He knew that some fans, teammates, and yes, some family members didn't want him to play with a black man," he said. "But my father listened to his heart and not to the chorus."

OUTSTANDING INFIELD

For several years, Pee Wee Reese and Jackie Robinson were Dodgers double-play partners at shortstop and second base. More than 25 years later, shortstop Alan Trammell and second baseman Lou Whitaker played the same role for the Detroit Tigers. Neither man is in the Hall of Fame. But they may have been the most successful double-play duo in major league history. The teammates played side by side for 19 seasons. Between the two of them, they made a record 2,819 double plays. Twice, they each won Gold Glove Awards in the same season.

PICKING UP BUTCH

2004 • MIDDLEBURY, VERMONT, UNITED STATES

Sara Smith was a talented pole vaulter at Middlebury College in Vermont. But that was not her finest achievement at Middlebury. She reached greater heights in a surprising partnership. Smith teamed up with a man who was many years older than her and who was in a wheelchair.

Richard "Butch" Varno was born with cerebral palsy. He grew up as a huge sports fan. His condition prevented him from playing the games he loved. But it couldn't stop him from cheering. In fact, he's one of the most memorable people in the history of Middlebury athletics.

It all started back in 1960. Butch was 13 years old. His grandmother was a housekeeper at the college dormitories. One day she wheeled him from their home to a Middlebury football game, a mile away. But then it started snowing. Varno's grandmother had trouble pushing his wheelchair on the way back.

Luckily, a student named Roger Ralph was driving past. He stopped and offered Varno and his grandmother a ride. And ever since that day, Middlebury athletes have been driving Varno to home games. This tradition has lasted more than 50 years. Middlebury students simply call it "picking up Butch."

During football season, using a special van, basketball players pick up Varno. (He still lives near campus.) When basketball season rolls around, freshman football players do the honors. At basketball games, Varno usually sits right next to the team's bench. "He can hear our huddle," said coach Jeff Brown. "He can encourage our guys." In fact, Varno often gives a pre-game speech. It's usually something along the lines of "I love you guys!" Sometimes he is in the middle of the players' huddle before tip-off. The players all touch his head and shout, "One, two, three . . . together!"

Together, Middlebury students have touched Varno's life in countless ways. They visit him, read to him, talk with him about the day's news, and help him with his physical therapy. "These kids care what happens to me," says Varno. "I don't know where I'd be without them."

WISE WORDS

"The main ingredient of stardom is the rest of the team."
—John Wooden, Hall of Fame college basketball coach

That was especially true of Sara Smith. Varno has called her "my motivator . . . emotional leader . . . best friend." Smith spent lots of time with Varno. She helped him celebrate his 56th birthday. And she also organized a team of other students to help him. "We were just really good friends," said Smith. "I think just having mutual respect means a lot to somebody who doesn't always get it."

Smith's biggest role was as Varno's tutor. For 18 months, she helped him get ready to take his GED test. People who take the GED did not finish high school. If they pass the test, they earn certificates similar to high school diplomas.

To get ready for the GED, Smith helped Varno study various subjects. She even convinced state educators to let him take a spoken version of the test because writing is hard for him. It took Varno three days to finish the test. When he passed, Smith and other friends threw him a surprise graduation party. Someone found him a cap and gown to wear.

Varno appreciated Smith's time and help. And he was proud of himself. "People said I couldn't do things. 'He can't read. He can't write.' She helped me show them I could," explained Varno. "I think it was probably my greatest moment that, without Sara, I couldn't have done."

But if you talk to Smith and others from Varno's life over the years, they will all tell you the same thing. Varno has boosted them and their spirits just as much as they have helped him. Together, they make a great team.

FRANCIS AND EDDIE

It was almost time for Francis Ouimet to tee off. He was trying to qualify for the 1913 U.S. Open Golf Championship. But he had a problem. Where was his caddie?

Ouimet was 20 years old. He lived right across the street from The Country Club in Brookline,

Massachusetts, which was hosting the tournament. As a child, he had often sneaked onto the course to collect golf balls and play a hole or two. But his family didn't have enough money to be members. So even though he had won the state amateur championship, Ouimet didn't feel like he belonged in this group of world-class players. The tournament even included his golf hero, Harry Vardon. Vardon had won the British Open five times.

As Ouimet waited on the practice green that day, a 10-year-old boy ran up to him. Eddie Lowery was out of breath. He had skipped school and taken an eight-mile trolley ride to Brookline to bring Ouimet some bad news. Lowery's older brother, who was scheduled to be Ouimet's caddie, couldn't come. But Lowery had an idea. "I could caddie for you," he said.

"My bag is as big as you are," Ouimet replied.

"I can do it, Mr. Ouimet, really I can," Lowery insisted. "I can help you out there."

Ouimet had been a caddie himself. He knew that the teamwork between caddie and golfer can make a big difference. Caddies don't only carry bags. They also help choose golf clubs and decide how to play different golf courses and holes. And, perhaps most important, a good caddie can help calm a golfer's nerves. It was hard to believe a 10-year-old could do all that.

But Ouimet saw determination on Lowery's face. "All right then, Eddie. Let's go," he said. "Just please call me Francis."

As the two of them headed to the first tee, fans and players snickered. After all, Ouimet and Lowery might have been the most unlikely pairing ever in a major golf tournament. The little-known amateur and his four-foot-tall caddie made a strange duo.

Ouimet's first two shots were awful. Lowery told him, "Keep your head down, and I'll watch the ball. I've never lost a ball yet." Ouimet did as he was told. He hit a beautiful 225-yard shot that landed only 25

JACK AND JUNIOR

Jack Nicklaus won a record 18 major golf tournaments in his remarkable career. He did so with a number of different caddies. Nicklaus's last and most famous victory was in the 1986 Masters Tournament. Nicklaus shot an incredible score of 30 on the final nine holes—a course record. And at 46 years old, Nicklaus became the oldest-ever Masters champion. Best of all, he shared the moment with family. His caddie that weekend was his 24-year-old son, Jack Jr.

feet from the flag. "Eddie," he said, "I think you and I are going to be good friends."

Ouimet went on to qualify for the U.S. Open. And he did far more than that. Thanks to Lowery's help and companionship, he played the best golf of his life. It was a high-pressure tournament. Thousands of people were watching. On the second-to-last hole of the final round, Ouimet sank a 20-foot putt. That shot tied him with the two leaders. Three men would compete in an 18-hole playoff. The three players were Ouimet, his hero Vardon, and long-hitting Englishman Ted Ray. Almost nobody thought Ouimet could win.

The next day, a Country Club member talked to Ouimet on the practice green. "You ought to have somebody carrying your bag who really knows the game and the course," he said. He said that he had offered Lowery five dollars—quite a bit of money in those days—to give up the job.

"I wouldn't do it for $100," said Lowery. He had tears in his eyes.

Ouimet just smiled. "I've already got the man I want on the bag."

By the time Ouimet tapped in his final putt on the 18th hole that day, he had beaten Vardon by five strokes. He beat Ray by six. It may have been golf's greatest upset. Hundreds of fans rushed toward Ouimet, lifting him on their shoulders. They also lifted Lowery, who was grinning from ear to ear. Later, the pair found a quiet moment by the gleaming U.S. Open trophy. The golfer turned to his caddie, who would become his lifelong friend. "I could not have done this without you," Ouimet told Lowery. "I think I was able to do what I did here because you believed I could."

GOLD-MEDAL MOM

2004 • ATHENS, GREECE

He has more gold medals than most people have pairs of socks. Many people view him as the greatest individual athlete in Olympic history. But swimmer Michael Phelps might never have reached such heights without his most valuable teammate: His mom.

Debbie Phelps knew her son was a good swimmer. By age 10, he was one of the top U.S. swimmers in his age group. But at the same time, he struggled at school. Phelps always seemed to be full of energy. He had trouble concentrating. He asked tons of questions and talked nonstop. "He was always pushing, nudging, shoving, and fidgeting," his mother explained. "It was hard for him to listen unless it was something that really captivated his attention."

When Phelps was in fifth grade, doctors diagnosed him with attention deficit hyperactivity disorder (ADHD). ADHD was what made it hard for him to focus. So his mother teamed up with him. Teachers kept telling Debbie all the things her son couldn't do. But she wanted to know what he *could* do. Together, mother and son simply focused on how he could overcome the challenges he faced. "I knew that, if I collaborated with Michael, he could achieve anything he set his mind to," she said.

When Phelps complained that he hated reading, his mother gave him the sports section of the newspaper. She found books about sports for him to read. When Phelps's attention strayed from math, she hired a tutor. She also suggested using word problems that would interest him. For example, "How long would it take to swim 500 meters if you swim three meters per second?"

Sometimes Phelps had trouble focusing on the tasks he needed to do before going to swim practice

or playing with friends. So his mother posted a daily to-do list on the refrigerator. Debbie gave him stickers when he completed his responsibilities. "It was a fun way to help him focus," she said.

Over time, Phelps built self-discipline. Swimming was an important part of that development. Debbie believed the water helped calm her son. "Even if Michael's mind was all over the place, he could focus on going up and down the pool," she explained. "I think the pool became a safe haven where he could release his energy."

That energy translated into huge success. At the 2004 Summer Olympics in Athens, Greece, Phelps won eight gold medals. These days, a sports-centered math problem might ask, "If Michael Phelps wins an average of 8 medals at the Olympics every 4 years, how many medals will he win over the course of 12 years?"

When officials hung the first gold medal around Phelps's neck in Athens, he also got a bouquet of flowers. A laurel wreath was placed on his head. After watching the American flag rise as the National Anthem played, Phelps stepped off the winner's platform. He walked to the stands and handed the flowers and wreath to his mom. "All kids can fail us at times," said Debbie. "But if you work with them, nine times out of ten they'll make you proud."

FAITHFUL TEAMMATES

Asmahan "Azzy" Mansour loved playing soccer. And
she was proud to wear her team's uniform. Mansour,
11 years old, played for the Nepean Hotspurs Selects.
They were an under-12 girls team in Ottawa, Canada.
Like her teammates, Mansour wore the team colors—
red shirt, red shorts, red socks. She also wore a hijab.
This long, silky scarf is a traditional head covering
that many Muslim girls and women wear. Mansour's
hijab covered her head but not her face. Mansour put
it on every morning as an expression of her faith. On
game days, her scarf was red, to match her uniform.

One Sunday at a tournament in the province of
Quebec, Mansour's coach sent her in to play about five
minutes into a game. But a referee blew his whistle.
He pointed at Mansour and gestured that she should

remove her hijab. Then he pointed to the bench. Mansour was puzzled. So was her coach. What was the problem?

Soccer's international organization is the Fédération Internationale de Football Association. In English, that means the International Federation of Association Football. Usually people call the group FIFA. FIFA rules say that a player "shall not use equipment or wear anything . . . that could be dangerous to himself or another player." FIFA's rules don't say anything specifically about headscarves. But Quebec's Soccer Federation had sent a memo to its officials. It stated that "the wearing of the Islamic veil or any other religious item is not permitted." Unless Mansour removed her scarf, the referee wouldn't allow her on the field. She refused.

"I don't understand why I can't play," she said. "This is so sad. It's my religion."

Mansour's teammates and their coach, Louis Maneiro, were upset, too. They called the ruling ridiculous. Maneiro also pointed out that Mansour had played in two games the previous day. The referees hadn't said a word then.

People reacted to the decision with anger and confusion. The issue was about much more than soccer. It soon became a news story across Canada. A week later, the controversy reached England. The annual meeting of the International Football Association Board (IFAB) was taking place there.

The IFAB talked about Mansour's story. The issue had many angles. For one thing, many Muslim countries have teams whose players wear headscarves. And in the United States, soccer players are allowed to wear hijabs and other religious clothing. But the IFAB decided to back the Quebec Soccer Federation's decision.

The IFAB's ruling disappointed Mansour's teammates. But by then they had already made a decision of their own. They had decided not to play. As a form of protest that Sunday, they walked off the field as a team. Four other teams at the tournament also forfeited their games in a show of support for Mansour. The act of solidarity got the attention of John Baird. At that time, Baird was Canada's Minister of the Environment.

"I was tremendously proud of the way the team and the coach handled the situation," he said.

Still, Mansour was sad for her fellow Nepean Hotspurs. She told a reporter, "I'm sorry my team couldn't play. It's my fault." But her teammates immediately came to their forward's defense. They told her, "We chose to leave, and that's a good thing." One player, Lisa Furano, said, "We supported our teammates and our friend."

KICKING FOR A CAUSE

In 2011, 15-year-old Shana McLaughlin was diagnosed with Hodgkin's lymphoma, a form of cancer. McLaughlin was a junior varsity soccer player. Her teammates at New Jersey's Chatham High School wanted to show their support. They decided to hold a fundraising tournament. They organized Chatham's boys' and girls' teams into three coed soccer teams and charged $5 for tickets. Many people in the community donated food to sell at the tournament. There were also baskets of purple gear for sale. (Purple is the color used for Hodgkin's lymphoma awareness.) All the money they earned went to an organization called the Emmanuel Cancer Foundation. The name of the soccer tournament, of course, was Shana's Cup.

TOUCHING TOUCHDOWN

OCTOBER 28, 2011 • LANCASTER, OHIO, UNITED STATES

Sometimes teammates can make a wish come true for a friend. And sometimes the *other* team can help, too.

Trent Glaze is a football fanatic. He always wanted to play the game. He dreamed about the thrill of cradling the ball and powering into the end zone for a touchdown. But Glaze has muscular dystrophy. It weakens the muscles and makes it hard to move. The disease makes his football dreams impossible. Glaze needs to use a wheelchair to get around. "Many times, I would sit in my room and just think, *Why me?* But then I said, well, if it's going to be me, then I'll just have to adapt," he explained.

One way Glaze adapted was by getting as close to football as he could without being a player. Glaze was a student at Fairfield Union High in Lancaster, Ohio.

As a sophomore, he became a team manager for the school's Falcons football team. Glaze studied the game closely. He went to each practice and team event. He learned every aspect of football. He was good at motivating the players, who became his friends. During games, he even recognized plays the other team was setting up and called them out to the team.

"He's my right-hand man," said Falcons head coach Tom McCurdy. "He's always telling me what we need to do, what needs to improve."

Glaze's senior year was in 2011. Coach McCurdy wanted to show his thanks to "Big T," as everyone called Glaze. So he made him a full-fledged member of the football team. He also named him team captain. "He deserves it," said the coach. "The way he approaches the game of life and the game of football is the right way of doing it." Glaze's mother, Debbie, added that the football team's support "just means the world to him."

Glaze's non-football classmates liked him, too. They named him homecoming king during football season. It was quite an honor. But it wasn't Glaze's biggest dream. *That* came true two weeks later.

The Falcons were playing a home game against Teays Valley High School. That night, many people in the crowd wore "Big T" shirts. Three times during the game, they yelled, "We want Trent! We want Trent!" Glaze just turned and smiled.

When the game ended, both teams stayed on the field. They lined up for a play. "I guess it was my time

GRAND FINALE

Jason McElwain was manager of the Greece Athena High School basketball team in Rochester, New York. Though he loved the game, McElwain—who was born with autism— was not a player. His job was to help run drills and hand out water. But in the last game of the team's 2006 regular season, the 17-year-old got the chance to be a star. The teamwork of his coaches and teammates gave him that chance. Coach Jim Johnson had decided to give the senior a parting gift. So with only a few minutes left, he sent McElwain into the game. McElwain missed his first two shots. But his teammates kept feeding him the ball. Then he sank a long one. And then another . . . and another. The crowd started going wild. In all, McElwain sank seven baskets, including six three-pointers. He scored an amazing 20 points! When the buzzer sounded, the crowd stormed the court. McElwain's teammates lifted him onto their shoulders. "I ended my career on the right note," said McElwain.

to shine," said Glaze. He wheeled himself out to the five-yard line and took a handoff from the quarterback. The ball slipped away at first. But another teammate picked it up and handed it back to Glaze, who rolled with it into the end zone.

Glaze's teammates and fans flooded onto the field. They hugged him and celebrated—even though they had just finished a winless season. Even the other team cheered! It was an amazing night for Glaze, who hopes to become a coach himself. "It's going to be in my memory for the rest of my life," said Glaze. "I'll never forget it."

DEEP SIX

JUNE 11, 2003 • NEW YORK, NEW YORK, UNITED STATES

Once in a while, personal glory is a team effort. During the 2003 baseball season, six Houston Astros pitchers made history. And they did it in one of the most famous arenas in sports—Yankee Stadium.

Houston's starting pitcher was Roy Oswalt. Eventually he'd be an all-star. But at the time, he was just 25 years old. In that game, he struck out the first three New York Yankees that he faced. But in the second inning, he was injured.

Oswalt's injury put Astros manager Jimy Williams in an unusual position. He had to turn to his bullpen for a relief pitcher early in the game. He called up Pete Munro, who was three days short of his 28th birthday. Over nearly three innings of work, Munro allowed three walks. But he didn't allow a single hit or a run.

With two outs in the fourth inning, 24-year-old Kirk Saarloos took the mound for Houston.

Roy Oswalt, who was injured in the second inning

Saarloos would play for a different team the next year. And he would end his career with a losing record (29–30). But that evening, he finished out the fourth and fifth innings without allowing a base runner. Next, Brad Lidge, a former first round draft pick, pitched perfect sixth and seventh innings. Then pitcher Octavio Dotel entered the game. He knew a no-hitter was on the line. It was his job to strike out every batter he faced.

Dotel now holds the record of playing for 13 different teams over the course of his career. But in this game, he matched another record. He struck out four batters in one inning. The unusual feat happened because Alfonso Soriano swung and missed on strike three. But the pitch got past Houston catcher Brad Ausmus. So Soriano was able to reach first base. Dotel struck out the inning's other three batters, too.

For the ninth inning, Williams brought in hard-throwing left-hander Billy Wagner. Wagner was on his way to setting the team record for saves in a season (44). But when he stepped to the mound, all he could think was: *Oh, my goodness, I have a shot to finish the no-hitter—at Yankee Stadium.* "There's no greater place to be part of history," he said.

It had been a team effort to get the Astros this far. It took teamwork not only by the pitchers, but also by the Houston defense. In the third inning, third baseman Geoff Blum made a bare-handed pickup on a slow ground ball. He threw out the runner at first base. Two innings later, left fielder Lance Berkman made a diving catch to prevent a single.

DIFFERENT DOUBLE PLAY

A double play in baseball takes first-rate teamwork, great timing, and lots of practice. And every double play is different. In a minor league game on May 26, 2011, Connecticut's New Britain Rock Cats turned one for the record books. The batter hit a ground ball to the first baseman. He threw home to the catcher. The catcher tossed it to the shortstop, and he threw to the pitcher. The pitcher hurled the ball to the third baseman, who tagged a runner for the first out. Then the third baseman threw back to the first baseman, who threw to the second baseman, who tossed it back to the shortstop. The shortstop threw the ball to the centerfielder covering second base, and he tagged another runner for a second out. Seven fielders—one double play.

Oswalt, Munro, Saarloos, Lidge, and Dotel watched nervously from the visitors' dugout. Wagner faced the final three batters. He struck out the first one. He struck out the next one. New York's last hope, slugger Hideki Matsui, came to the plate. But he grounded out weakly to first base to end the game—an 8–0 victory for Houston. Wagner pumped his fist in celebration. It was the first time six men had ever combined for a no-hitter in the big leagues. It was also the first time in more than 50 years that New York had been no-hit in Yankee Stadium.

New York had lost, but the home fans gave the visiting team a standing ovation. They knew a remarkable feat when they saw it. Surely it would never happen again. But guess what? Only nine years later, six Seattle Mariners pitchers did the exact same thing against the Los Angeles Dodgers!

PUPPY LOVE

MARCH 14, 1990 • NOME, ALASKA, UNITED STATES

Susan Butcher had just raced through the Alaskan wilderness for 1,151 frostbitten miles. She was tired and cold. But she was happy. Wearing a bright red snowsuit and a wide smile, she trotted across the finish line of the Iditarod Trail Sled Dog Race. And she did it with the team that it made it possible—her dogs.

The Iditarod is a demanding event. In it, sled dog racers drive teams of specially trained dogs.

Sled dog racers are also called mushers. During the Iditarod, mushers go through blizzards, over mountain ranges, and across frozen seas. They travel between the cities of Anchorage and Nome. The race is a test of endurance for both the humans and their furry companions. The 1990 race was especially hard for the 70 teams that started it. That year, mushers had to deal with the deepest snow in 25 years. They also ran into ash from a volcano and even the occasional aggressive moose or herd of buffalo. Fortunately, Butcher and her team of dogs had been preparing for the challenge since birth.

WISE WORDS

"In order to have a winner, the team must have a feeling of unity; every player must put the team first—ahead of personal glory."
—Paul "Bear" Bryant, Hall of Fame college football coach

Butcher was from Massachusetts. When she was little, her parents got divorced. It was a hard time for Butcher. But she found comfort in four-legged friends. "I was born with a particular ability with animals and a particular love for them," she said. "An animal loves you, and you love them. I needed that as a child."

Butcher later became a veterinary technician. She also raised dogs called huskies. Eventually, her work led her to Alaska. She moved to a tiny town called Eureka. It had a population of six people.

Two of those six residents were Butcher and her husband, David Monson. Monson was also a dog racer. In Eureka, the couple lived in a log cabin. They didn't have running water, flush toilets, or a TV. But they had lots of dogs. They raised huskies with names such as Sluggo, Elan, and Hermit. There were nearly 150 of them in Butcher's Trail Breaker Kennel.

Butcher's personal bond with the dogs started the minute they were born. She held each tiny puppy in her hands and breathed into its nose. That way, the animal would always associate her smell with comfort. She fed the dogs, trained them, and massaged them after long runs. She let a few of them sleep in the cabin each night. Once she even stayed up for five nights in a row with a sick dog named Granite. Butcher held Granite's head in her lap until he got better. Eventually he became, according to Butcher, one of the best sled dogs ever.

Butcher won the 1990 Iditarod in record time. It took her and her team of dogs 11 days, 1 hour, 53 minutes, and 23 seconds. The victory was her fourth in five years, making her one of the sport's all-time greats. She would eventually join the Alaska Sports Hall of Fame.

In 2006, at age 51, Butcher died of leukemia. However, she still has a place in the world of sled dog racing. The Iditarod begins on the first Saturday of every March. That day is now officially Susan Butcher Day in Alaska.

The Iditarod crowns an individual champion. But Butcher knew that she shared credit for the success. "This team has been absolutely incredible," she said after that fourth triumph. "I've never had a team go as strong as this." The secret? Butcher said, "It must be the combination working together."

THE PLAY

NOVEMBER 20, 1982 • BERKELEY, CALIFORNIA, UNITED STATES

In a thrilling game between two college football rivals, desperation led to teamwork.

Since 1892, Stanford University and the University of California, Berkeley, have been competing against each other on the football field. Their rivalry is intense, but also good-natured. Over the years, pranks surrounding the Cal-Stanford game have been nearly as famous as the game itself. In 1949, students from each school flew planes over the other's campus. They dropped leaflets about how their team was going to crush the other in "The Big Game." The next year, the Stanford band went to San Francisco dressed in their rival's colors. They spent hours playing the University of California's fight song—purposely off-key.

But in 1982, the Stanford band played a role in The Big Game's outcome. In that contest, several Cal players worked together to create one of the most famous

moments in sports history. It was a series of events known simply as "The Play."

The 85th meeting between Cal and Stanford was a classic. The lead changed hands several times. With only four seconds left, Stanford kicked a field goal. It gave them a 20–19 lead. Several Stanford players rushed onto the field, thinking the game was over. But it wasn't. So officials gave Stanford a penalty. They had to kick off from their own 25-yard line. Cal's special teams captain, Richard Rodgers, talked with his teammates. He told them, "If you get the ball and you're gonna be tackled, pitch it. Don't fall with the ball."

California's Kevin Moen received the kickoff on his own 43-yard line. He took the ball five yards before tossing it to Rodgers. Rodgers ran a few yards and then tossed it to Dwight Garner. As Garner was tackled, he pitched the ball back to Rodgers. Many people thought Garner's knee touched the turf before he let go of the ball. That would mean the game was over. But the referees didn't call it. Even so, the Stanford band started celebrating.

The band streamed onto the field. Meanwhile, Rodgers crossed the 50-yard line. Then he tossed a sideways pass to teammate Mariet Ford. "Once I got it, I just took off," Ford recalled. But Ford could only make it to the 25-yard line. Then he was about to be tackled. So he took a chance. He just threw the ball blindly over his right shoulder—right to Moen, who had received the kickoff in the first place.

By now, the Stanford band was all over the field. But Moen kept running. "I grabbed the ball, but didn't really see the goal line," he later said. "All I saw was the band. As far as I was concerned, they were all Stanford players, and I just busted through them." He finally made it into the end zone. There he barreled into a very surprised trombone player. When officials finally signaled the touchdown, Cal radio announcer Joe Starkey put it best. He called it "the most amazing, sensational, heartrending, exciting, thrilling finish in the history of college football!"

As for that unfortunate trombone player, his crumpled instrument became famous. It's on display at the College Football Hall of Fame.

AN UNEXPECTED DUO

APRIL 25, 2003 • PORTLAND, OREGON, UNITED STATES

Of all days to be fighting the flu, Natalie Gilbert thought, *why this day?* "You can stay home," her parents told her. "You don't have to do it." But how could she not? This was supposed to be her shining moment.

At 13 years old, Gilbert was a talented singer. In fact, her singing had won a contest. The prize? Singing the National Anthem before Game 3 of the 2003 NBA Western Conference quarterfinals. Nearly 20,000 people were in the stands. And a national TV audience was watching at home.

Gilbert was well prepared to perform. She had even practiced the song in a locker room a few minutes before show time. But she had been in bed much of the day.

Now Gilbert took a deep breath and walked to center court. Microphone in hand, she started singing. She got through the first part without trouble. "Oh, say can you see by the dawn's early light what so proudly we hailed . . ." But then she simply stopped.

"The words went out the window," Gilbert explained later. "I had no idea what to do."

The crowd tried to cheer her on. But she was flustered. She closed her eyes. She put her hand to her forehead. Nothing. Wearing a pained expression, she looked around for help.

ANTHEM AID

On January 7, 2011, eight-year-old Elizabeth Hughes had the thrill of her life. She sang the National Anthem before a minor league hockey game in Florida. She made it through the first minute of the song beautifully. But right after she sang the words "gave proof," the sound system stopped working. All was quiet for a few seconds. Then a big moment of natural teamwork happened. The crowd—and the players on both teams—simply raised their voices. They sang the anthem louder than ever, helping Hughes finish the job.

She got the help she was looking for. And it came from an unexpected person. Maurice Cheeks, head coach of the Portland Trail Blazers, stepped up. "Mo" Cheeks had been a four-time NBA all-star guard. He was known for his unselfish play. When he retired, he was ranked fifth all-time in career assists. And now he was going to offer a very memorable assist.

"She looked helpless, and I just started walking," Cheeks recalled. "As I approached her, I just wanted to help her." He added, "I didn't know if I even knew all the words."

"C'mon, c'mon," he gently said to Gilbert. "Starlight's last gleaming . . ." Gilbert repeated the phrase. "Whose broad stripes and bright stars . . ." he continued, his hand resting on her shoulder. She sang that, too.

As Cheeks sang along with her, Gilbert hit her stride. The words came out strong. The coach continued to sing with her. His voice? Well . . . let's just say he should stick to basketball. But that didn't matter to Gilbert. All that mattered was his support.

"And the rockets' red glare, the bombs bursting in air . . ."

The teamwork between Cheeks and Gilbert inspired the fans, players, and coaches. So *they* all raised their voices, too. It was a louder-than-usual performance of the National Anthem. And it was one the crowd would definitely remember.

By the time Gilbert belted out, "And the land of the free . . ." in perfect pitch, Cheeks was smiling down at her. And the crowd was cheering wildly. When the song was over, the coach gave Gilbert a hug. "He totally saved me," said Gilbert, who still sings and plays piano today.

One year later, the Philadelphia 76ers flew Gilbert to the East Coast to sing the anthem before another game. The 76ers opponent: the Trail Blazers. Once again, Cheeks stood nearby as Gilbert sang. But this time, he didn't need to help her. She nailed it.

TOGETHER AT THE TOP OF THE WORLD

MAY 29, 1954 • THE HIMALAYAN MOUNTAINS, NEPAL AND TIBET

Mountain climbing is an adventure sport. But that doesn't mean it's all fun and games. On the world's tallest mountains, it can be deadly serious. Climbers face many risks. They can get altitude sickness from being so high above sea level. The great height makes it hard for the body to get enough oxygen. So climbers may feel dizzy, have trouble breathing, faint, or even die. Mountain climbers also face other dangers. They can freeze in the bitterly cold temperatures. Or they can fall thousands of feet.

Mount Everest is one of the greatest challenges for climbers. At 29,028 feet, it's the highest peak on the planet. It sits on the border between Nepal and Tibet in the Himalayan Mountains. Hundreds of people have died trying to climb it.

Because the mountain is so dangerous, most climbing teams hire Sherpas. Sherpas are people who live near Mount Everest. They get used to the high altitudes more quickly than most people. They help climbing teams figure out routes to the peak.

In 1953, the British Everest Expedition set out to climb the great mountain. The team had many skilled mountaineers. It also included 20 Sherpa guides. In addition, the team had 362 porters to carry supplies and 10,000 pounds of baggage.

The first part of the expedition was months of very careful planning. Next came seven weeks of climbing to nine camps. Each camp was higher than the last. The slow progress helped the climbers get used to the altitude. Finally, expedition leader John Hunt chose two pairs of men to head for the summit.

The first two men got pretty close. They made it within 300 vertical feet of the top. But then they ran into bad weather and problems with their oxygen tanks. They had to turn back.

The second team was Edmund Hillary and Tenzing Norgay. Hillary was a climber from New Zealand. He was 33 years old. Tenzing, a Sherpa, was 39. (In some Asian nations, family names come before individual names. So Tenzing's personal name is "Norgay" and

GOING DOWN

In 2009, 55 years after Hillary and Tenzing reached Earth's highest point, another team traveled far below Earth's surface. These explorers were six students from Sheffield University in England. They were the first people to explore and map a huge network of caves. These caves were on the Greek island of Crete. The students worked in two groups. While one group slept, the other went down into cramped shafts and dangerous tunnels. If an accident happened, there was no hope of rescue. The mouth of the cave was seven hours away from the nearest village. The deepest cave the group explored was more than 1,500 feet below the surface. The round-trip took about 16 hours!

his family name is "Tenzing.") Tenzing had tried six times to reach Everest's peak. But he and his climbing partners had never made it.

Tenzing had already shown his skill, though. Earlier in the British Everest Expedition's climb, Hillary was moving supplies up to one of the camps. Suddenly the ice gave way. Hillary fell into a deep crack. Tenzing was following right behind, tied to the same rope. He thought fast and shoved his ice axe into the snow. Then he whipped the rope around it and tightened it—just in time to save Hillary. The New Zealander decided then that this Sherpa would be his best climbing partner. He was right. They became a world-famous team.

At 6:30 a.m. on May 29, the two men began the last part of the climb. The hardest stretch was a sheer 40-foot rock face. It's now known as the Hillary Step. But together, Hillary and Tenzing made it past each challenge. Exactly five hours after setting out that morning, the duo reached the highest point on Earth.

Hillary reached out to shake Tenzing's hand. He got a hug instead.

Over the next several decades, hundreds of people from all over the globe would match this feat. But as far as anyone knows, Hillary and Tenzing were the first. They conquered a mountain that some thought was impossible to conquer.

Later, Tenzing said that Hillary was the first person to actually set foot on the peak. But the only photo of their success shows Tenzing holding an ice axe and standing at the top of the world. (Because of low oxygen, the men could only spend a few minutes at the summit.) After they came down from the mountain, they did many interviews. Reporters asked again and again which of the two men reached the summit first. Hillary shrugged off the question. He replied that the achievement belonged to them both equally. As Hunt put it, "They reached it together, as a team."

PRICELESS DIAMOND

APRIL 14, 2010 • INDIANAPOLIS, INDIANA, UNITED STATES

It was an April afternoon in 2010. The John Marshall Community High School girls' softball team showed up to play the freshman team from Roncalli High School. Roncalli coaches thought it might be a mismatch. And it was. But it also turned out to be a *perfect* match.

Roncalli was a private school in Indianapolis. Its softball team, the Rebels, hadn't lost a game in over two years. Marshall was a middle school that was changing to include high school students. And its team, the Patriots, was playing its first softball game ever. Marshall showed up with only two bats, just a few good gloves, no helmets, and no cleats. The team had only practiced a handful of times. And those practices had been on a field with trees growing in the outfield. Sixteen of the girls had never played the game before. They didn't know where to stand in the batter's box. They asked questions like, "How should I hold the bat?" and "Which one is first base?"

In the game's first two innings, Marshall pitchers walked nine batters. At that point, the teams' coaches talked. They discussed stopping the game and simply focusing on teaching the girls the basics of softball. The undefeated Roncalli team even offered to forfeit the game. Instead, Marshall decided to forfeit. That's when the two competing teams took the field as one.

The experienced Roncalli girls introduced themselves to the Marshall players. Then the Roncalli Rebels started teaching the Patriots some basic softball skills. They showed them how to pitch, field, and run the bases. They also demonstrated how to put on catching gear, the right way to stand at bat, and more. The Marshall girls were thrilled and thankful. They high-fived and hugged their new friends.

"Our girls made me as proud as I've ever been," said Roncalli junior varsity coach Jeff Traylor. "You could tell they were having a blast. The change from the beginning of the game to the end of practice was amazing."

TIE GAME

Teamwork between two opponents can mean whole teams sharing equipment. Or it can mean one player helping an opposing player with one piece of equipment. In 2013, that happened during a soccer match between two Saudi Arabian teams. Goalkeeper Taisir Al Antaif received a pass from a teammate. He prepared to kick the ball away from the goal. But the laces on his shoe had come untied. He was wearing large gloves, so he couldn't tie his shoe. And if he kicked the ball, his shoe was likely to go flying, too. That's when an opposing player named Jóbson stepped in. (His full name is Jóbson Leandro Pereira de Oliveira, but fans just call him Jóbson.) He could have stolen the ball. Instead, he squatted down and tied the goalkeeper's cleats for him. Then the two players high-fived. The referee gave Jóbson's team a free kick, but they didn't think that was fair. So they just rolled the ball out of bounds. Fittingly, the game ended in a tie.

Afterward, Traylor sent a letter to the parents of Roncalli students. He asked for donations to help the Marshall program. "I have some ideas of some great things we can do for these kids," he wrote. "I think every one of them deserves to have their own bats, gloves, cleats, sliders, batting gloves, helmets, all of it."

Traylor's message spread beyond the Roncalli community. The response was huge! People all over the country were inspired by the teamwork between the two teams. They sent emails of support. But they did more than that. They also sent money and lots of softball equipment. The owner of an indoor batting cage offered Marshall's team free practice time at the cage in the winter. The Cincinnati Reds baseball team donated good dirt for a new field at Marshall.

Later, Roncalli invited Marshall back for another practice. This time, the Rebels gave the Patriots new gloves, batting helmets, and just about every piece of equipment they might need. And the Marshall team was eager to try out their new skills. "The Marshall players wanted to show us everything they had learned," said Traylor. "And they wanted to learn more."

But Traylor knows that his players learned something, too. "We win a lot of games," he explained. "But this time, it was bigger than winning, bigger than the game."

BETTER TOGETHER

AUGUST 1, 2010 • LOS ANGELES, CALIFORNIA, UNITED STATES

Identical twins Mike and Bob Bryan have always done lots of things together. When they were six years old, they both made it to the finals of a tennis tournament. But they were supposed to play against each other— not together. Their parents, who are tennis teachers, wouldn't let that happen. They had the brothers flip a coin instead. "We brought home the winner and runner-up trophies," said Mike.

From then on, the talented brothers kept rising through the junior tennis ranks. They also continued to avoid playing against each other. They simply took turns stepping down from tournaments if they were scheduled to face off. One brother would give up his chance so that the other brother could move on. "We were always careful to have the boys not feel competitive," their father, Wayne, explained. "Which," he added, "in an individual sport is very hard to do."

As the years passed, Mike and Bob took turns winning titles in every age group. Eventually they turned professional. At their peak as pro singles players, they were very good. But they weren't great. Bob's top world ranking was 116th. Mike's was 246th. As teammates, however, they were almost unstoppable. In fact, the Bryan brothers may be the greatest men's doubles pair in tennis history. In 2010, they won the Farmers Classic in Los Angeles. With that victory, they broke the record for most doubles tournament titles on the Association of Tennis Professionals (ATP) Tour. At the time, that record was 62. Since that tournament, the brothers have won many more titles.

There's a friendly joke on the tennis tour that the twins have an unfair advantage. Other players say that even if doubles partners played together for their entire lives, they would still have nine months less experience than the Bryans. It's true that for years the brothers were nearly inseparable. As small children, they often climbed into bed together. When they went to Stanford University, they were assigned separate dorm rooms. But Bob chose to sleep on a mattress in Mike's room for the rest of the year.

On the court, the twins are the same in many ways. Both use one-handed backhands. Both have smooth ground strokes. But there are differences, too. Mike is right-handed. Bob is a lefty. Mike is faster on his feet and better at returning serves. Bob has a better serve and a stronger forehand. Mike is two minutes older. At 6-foot-4 and 202 pounds, Bob is about an inch taller and 10 pounds heavier. Mike is allergic to wheat. Bob can eat anything.

The key to the Bryan brothers' success is their connection on the court. They don't say much to each other during matches. In fact, they talk less during games than most doubles teams do. But they know exactly what to do. Each one can predict just where his brother will be and where he will hit the ball.

The Bryans like to celebrate winning points with chest bumps. And they just keep winning . . . and winning . . . and winning. They have set a tour record for most match victories. They also set tour records for the longest run as the top-ranked doubles team and for most Grand Slam finals appearances in a row. (The four Grand Slam tournaments are Wimbledon, the U.S. Open, the French Open, and the Australian Open.)

The ATP named them the Team of the Decade for 2000–2009. But the brothers didn't stop when the decade ended. They earned a gold medal at the 2012 Olympic Games in London, England. And their victory at the 2013 Wimbledon Championships made the Bryans the first men's doubles team to win all four Grand Slam tournaments in a row.

Athletes never know quite what to expect from the future. But the Bryans know one thing for sure. As Mike said, "We know, wherever we're going, we do it together."

SENSATIONAL SISTERS

Venus and Serena Williams are two of the best female tennis players ever. Each has spent time as the top-ranked player in the world. By the end of the 2013 season, they had won a total of 24 Grand Slam singles titles (17 by Serena and 7 by Venus). Unlike the Bryan brothers, some of the sisters' most famous matches have been against each other. But like the Bryans, the sisters are also a doubles powerhouse. As partners, they have won 13 Grand Slam doubles titles. They have also teamed up to win three Olympic gold medals.

UNIFORM SUPPORT

2011 • HOPKINS, MICHIGAN, UNITED STATES

As a soccer player, Keara Kilbane was a star. Playing for her high school in Michigan, she was a three-time all-district and all-conference player. However, the 17-year-old athlete didn't know much about football. So when Hopkins High football coach Glenn Noble asked her if she would like to try out for his team, she thought he was kidding. But Noble was totally serious. "I want to see if you can kick a football the way you kick a soccer ball," he said. Kilbane said she would give it a shot.

Kilbane's tryout for the team was supposed to be private. But several of the boys on the Hopkins Vikings football squad secretly watched from the locker room. They were curious. A girl? On the football team?

Actually, female players on high school foot-ball teams are becoming more and more common. Nearly three dozen girls play football each season in

Michigan alone. But it had never happened at
Hopkins High.

When Kilbane went to try out, she wasn't sure
how to kick the football. In soccer, you want to boot
the lower third of the ball to get some lift. In football,
you don't. Kilbane wasn't sure exactly where to kick
the ball from, either. "Do I kick it on the ground?" she
asked. "In the air?" The coaches showed her the right
way to kick. And then she showed them what she
could do. "She came out and pretty much amazed
us," said Noble. "She has great distance and near-
perfect accuracy."

Next the coaches met
with Kilbane and her
parents. They asked
if she would like

to be the Vikings' kicker. Kilbane's parents, Brian and Paula, were a little worried about the idea. They thought playing football might be dangerous. Plus, their daughter was already busy with many other responsibilities, including being senior class president. "I advised her not to do it," said her mom. "But we always let our kids make the final decision." Kilbane decided to leave it up to the boys who might become her teammates. "If the guys didn't want me there," she said, "I wouldn't do it."

Hopkins athletic director Scott Van Bonn was worried about that, too. How would the team react to Kilbane? What about the boys who had wanted to be kicker? What about the players who had been practicing so hard? How would they respond?

As it turned out, Van Bonn didn't need to worry. "Our football boys have been phenomenal with her," he said. "They've taken her on like a little sister. The boys responded in exactly the right way."

The Vikings had good reason to welcome Kilbane. She was proud to put on her blue and white uniform and tuck her long blond hair into a helmet. And she devoted herself to the team. In the whole 2011 season, she missed only two extra points. "None of us can kick as well as her," said middle linebacker Joe Lodenstein. Tight end Tyler Schwartz agreed. "She's one of us," he said. And team quarterback Mitchel Pavlak adds, "She's one of the most dedicated members of the team. She deserves our respect."

Kilbane, who plans to attend medical school, is just as happy with her teammates. "It's been the best experience ever," she said. "All the guys have been unbelievably supportive." But what about guys on other teams? Pavlak worried that opponents might hassle Kilbane on the field. "But," he said, smiling, "if they did, they'd have 46 other kids all over them."

PRACTICED PERFECTION

MARCH 28, 1992 • PHILADELPHIA, PENNSYLVANIA, UNITED STATES

Precision is a big part of great teamwork. When a team practices enough together, the most impossible-seeming plays become possible—even in high-pressure situations.

The East Regional finals of the 1992 NCAA men's basketball tournament were definitely high-pressure. The first round of play, called the Sweet Sixteen, was over. It had led to an Elite Eight matchup between two of college basketball's best teams. One, the University of Kentucky Wildcats, had already won five national titles. The other, Duke University's Blue Devils, were trying to reach their fifth Final Four in a row. After the Final Four, the last step was the championship.

With 11 minutes left in the second half of the Elite Eight game, Duke was leading by 12 points. Kentucky coach Rick Pitino called a timeout. "We have them right where we want them," he told his players. "Now we make our comeback." The Wildcats scored the next eight points. The half ended in a tie, and the game went into overtime.

The last 32 seconds of overtime were dizzyingly dramatic. In those few moments, the lead changed hands five times. Every basket seemed like it would be the game-winner. With only 2.2 seconds left, Kentucky's Sean Woods made a shot. It gave his team a 103–102 edge, and Wildcat fans began celebrating. But it *still* wasn't over. Duke quickly called a timeout. Coach Mike Krzyzewski set up one final, daring play. It involved two players who would go on to become professional stars—Grant Hill and Christian Laettner.

Only 2.1 seconds were left in the game. The clock wouldn't start again until a player touched the ball inbounds. So Hill, the son of a former Dallas Cowboys running back, had to act more like a quarterback than a hoops player. He needed to make a very long pass. From under his own basket, he would throw the ball nearly three-quarters of the court to Laettner. Laettner would run from the left corner to the foul line and catch the ball. Then he just had to take the best shot possible before the final buzzer.

"Grant, can you make the pass?" Krzyzewski asked. "Yeah, Coach," he answered. "I can do it."

"Can you catch it?" the coach asked Laettner. Laettner nodded.

SIZING THEM UP

Teamwork can mean coming up big for your teammates by doing the little things well. On the 1987–1988 Washington Bullets basketball team, that was true—literally. That year, the team included 5-foot-3 rookie Muggsy Bogues—the shortest player in NBA history. One of his teammates was 7-foot-7 second-year player Manute Bol—the tallest NBA player. The duo got a lot of publicity for their mismatched size and posed for many dramatic photographs. But the hype wasn't as important as their performance. Neither scored many points. But Bogues led the team in assists, and Bol led in blocked shots. Together, they showed that the most important measurement was the size of their contributions.

Earlier that season, Hill had tried a similar pass to Laettner. But in that game, the ball sailed too wide. It ended up out of bounds. This time, Hill sent the ball flying straight to Laettner. Laettner leaped, grabbed it, and somehow came down without losing his balance. He dribbled once and faked to his right. Then he spun left, jumped, and released a 17-foot shot—just before the buzzer sounded.

Up to that point, Laettner hadn't missed a shot all night. He'd made nine of nine shots from the floor. He had also made all 10 of his free throws. Could he finish off a perfect evening?

Swish! Joy on the court. Duke 104, Kentucky 103.

More than 260 sports writers were at that game. Most agreed it was one of the best college basketball games they had ever seen. And in that game, two teammates were connected in basketball history forever. "The pass and the catch were perfect. If a guy hits a home run or sinks a hole in one, that's one play," said Krzyzewski. "When two people make a great play, it's more worthy of disbelief."

BUTTERFLIES IN LANE THREE

JULY 24, 2010 • AKRON, OHIO, UNITED STATES

At the 2010 Soap Box Derby, the spirit of teamwork shone brightly. And it did so in an unusual and inspiring way. It shone through a teammate who was there only in spirit.

For most of her life, Carol Anne Brown was an energetic, active girl. She lived in Spotsylvania,

Virginia. One of her passions was Soap Box Derby. In this sport, 8- to 17-year-olds build cars without motors. (Sometimes their parents help.) Then the Derby racers steer the cars carefully down a slope.

Brown dreamed of competing in the sport's world championships, the All-American Soap Box Derby. This race takes place every year in Akron, Ohio. She tried twice to qualify. Both times, she finished in second place. The second time, she lost by just two-hundredths of a second.

Brown did a lot more than Derby racing. She was a lacrosse player and a horseback rider. She was a cheerleader, an actress, a musician, and a volunteer. She also had bipolar disorder, a type of mental illness. The disorder became more serious around the time Brown started high school. It led to periods of great activity—and sometimes risky and unhealthy behaviors. These times would be followed by sudden plunges into depression. One weekend in 2009, that depression led to tragedy. At the age of 18, Brown took her own life.

The family was crushed. But they found some comfort in the fact that her tragic story might benefit others. Brown had signed up to be an organ donor. Her choice helped five different people. In addition, her parents, Todd and Michelle, created the website www.bipolaraware.org. They wanted the site to help others recognize the symptoms of bipolar disorder. Meanwhile, Brown's brother, Sean, drew inspiration from her memory.

Sean was an all-county wrestler, a soccer player, and a triathlete. He was also an honor roll student. And, like his sister, he was a pretty good Soap Box Derby racer. He had often finished in second place.

WISE WORDS

"Teamwork is the essence of life. It makes everything possible from moonshots to building cities to the renewal of life. And a good team multiplies the potential of everyone on it."

—Pat Riley, Hall of Fame basketball coach

But the year after Brown's death, 14-year-old Sean qualified for the world championships. The big race featured 556 competitors from around the world.

Sean competed in his sister's old car. Usually, a racer's name is painted on the car's side. Sean's car said "Sean & Carol Anne Brown." Inside, Sean taped up a photo of Carol Anne. "I knew she was there with me," he said.

Before Sean's first race in the Rally Super Stock Division, Michelle and Todd were sitting in the stands. As they waited, a white butterfly circled Michelle's head. Then the race started. Sean recorded the best time of the round—29.47 seconds. In the second round, Sean was .04 seconds faster. He won again in the third round.

In the championship heat, Sean was racing in the third of three lanes. Again, a white butterfly circled his family as they watched. Then it flew away and landed in lane three. The sign gave the Browns hope as the race began. Since that day, the Brown family has come

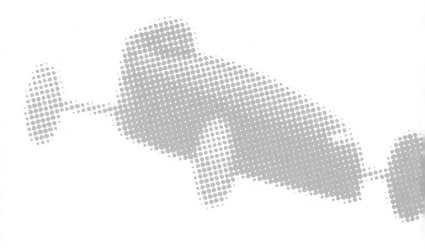

to view that butterfly as a symbol of their daughter and sister's presence. To them, it's a sign that she is still with them.

Less than 30 seconds after the race started, Sean was announced as the winner at the finish line. The Brown family had scattered Carol Anne's ashes there that morning.

After Sean won, a mob of family members crowded around to hug him. Later, Todd Brown talked about all of the things that led to Sean's triumph. "It was a combination of talent, setup, and luck," he said, "and his sister."

Suicide is a terrible way for anyone to die. If you ever feel like hurting yourself, tell an adult **right away.** Talk to a parent, a teacher, or any other adult you trust. Or call 911 or a crisis hotline such as 1-800-999-9999. **Don't wait. Get help.**

LIS AND JUBILEE

JULY 29, 1952 • HELSINKI, FINLAND

Around the world, thousands of people with special needs enjoy horseback riding. This is called therapeutic riding. Riding can help people who have physical or emotional disabilities. It can improve balance and strengthen muscles. Riders get to enjoy the outdoors. And some riders form relationships with their horses. That relationship can bring a lot of comfort.

One woman from Denmark is given credit for inspiring the practice of therapeutic riding. Actually, one woman and one very special horse.

At age 23, Lis Hartel was a star in the sport of horseback riding. This sport is also called equestrian. Hartel's event was dressage. In that event, the horse and rider memorize and perform a series of movements. It looks a lot like a dance. But one day in 1944, Hartel woke up with a headache and a stiff neck. Within a few days, a lot of her body was paralyzed. She had polio.

In the 1950s, doctors developed a vaccine for polio. But before that, the disease affected hundreds of thousands of people each year. It could be deadly. It also left many patients unable to walk properly. Doctors told Hartel she would probably never ride again.

However, Hartel was very determined. Soon, she got some movement back. She started to walk with crutches. From the knees down she was still paralyzed. Her arms, hands, and thighs also were weak. Yet only a year after being struck by polio, she was helped back onto a horse.

Hartel fell several times before learning how to balance properly without the full use of her legs. Soon, she felt comfortable on horseback again. And she was eager to get back to dressage training.

First, Hartel had to choose a horse. She picked out one named Jubilee. Jubilee was an ordinary-looking horse. But she was calm. Each time Hartel was lifted onto her, Jubilee stood as still as a statue. And she was dependable. Jubilee learned to respond to a different type of riding. Hartel couldn't use her legs to guide Jubilee. So instead, she gave the horse signals by shifting her weight. Dressage is all about harmony between the rider and the horse. Hartel and Jubilee quickly developed a very close bond.

Together, Hartel and Jubilee began to win events. Only three years after her polio attack, Hartel finished second in the riding championship of Scandinavia (Norway, Sweden, Finland, and Denmark). She soon began dreaming of competing in the Summer Olympics.

For many years, women were not allowed to compete in equestrian events at the Olympic Games.

RED'S RIDE

For a long time, Canadian jockey John "Red" Pollard couldn't win a race. Early in his career, a racing accident left him completely blind in his right eye. Guiding a thousand-pound horse with only one good eye was very dangerous. Pollard knew that if track officials found out, they wouldn't let him compete. So he kept it a secret.

Meanwhile, Pollard kept struggling as a jockey. In 1936, he went to the Michigan State Fairgrounds in Detroit. He didn't have enough money for the trip. So he hitched rides. In Detroit, he met a horse trainer. The trainer was looking for a jockey to ride Seabiscuit. He was a small, moody horse. And just like Pollard, he couldn't seem to win. He had lost his first 17 races.

When Pollard met Seabiscuit, he offered him a sugar cube. The usually unfriendly horse responded by affectionately touching Pollard's shoulder with his nose. It was as if he had chosen his jockey. The partnership turned both into champions. By the time Seabiscuit was retired from racing in 1940, he was the sport's all-time leading money winner.

All riders had to be male military officers. But by the 1952 Olympics in Helsinki, Finland, the rules had changed. That year, four women competed against 23 men in the dressage competition. One of those women was Hartel.

At the Olympics, Hartel still needed people to help her on and off Jubilee. But she rode with such grace that many spectators didn't realize she had a disability. In the end, she earned a silver medal. As soon as Hartel finished her event and the medals were announced, a gentleman rushed over to Jubilee's side. It was gold-medal-winner Henri Saint Cyr from Sweden. He carried Hartel to the victory platform for the medal presentation. After all Hartel had over-come, it was one of the most emotional moments in Olympic history.

Four years later, Hartel won another Olympic silver medal. Eventually, she became the first woman from Scandinavia inducted into the International Women's Sports Hall of Fame. But she also made history on that special day in 1952. Hartel was the first woman to share an Olympic medal podium with men. Jubilee didn't get to join her rider on the podium. But Hartel knew that she shared her victory with a special teammate.

BIG-HEARTED LITTLE LEAGUERS

2007 • BOULDER, COLORADO, UNITED STATES

Kyle Hernden was a Little Leaguer on an all-star team in Boulder, Colorado. In 2007, the 12-year-old was a pitcher, first baseman, and outfielder. Hernden always gave his best effort, and he was usually one of the first kids to show up for practice. His mother, Patty, was the treasurer of the South Boulder Little League. His father, Charlie, was a big fan of the game. Like many families around the country, the Herndens were a baseball family.

But Hernden's days were different from those of any other kid in the league. Every evening after practice, he went to see his dad. His dad wasn't at home. He was at a hospice. A hospice is a place where nurses care for sick people who can't be cured. Hernden's father was dying of cancer.

As Charlie got sicker, Hernden's coaches told him he could skip practices. They wanted him to take as much time away from the game as he needed. But in fact, the game was helping him get through this hard time. "I suppose that it was an escape for him," said Hernden's coach Mike Green.

CHANGE OF HEART

For Mike Green, coaching Kyle Hernden and his teammates was a turning point. Watching the players discover the power of pals and priorities gave him a different view. "This event truly changed my life and perspective on sports," he said.

Green didn't always have this perspective. Two years earlier he was coaching during an all-star game for 10-year-olds. And he had gotten mad. He threw his hat down in disgust at his team's poor performance. (Hernden was on that team, too.) Officials kicked Green out of the game. But thanks to the inspiration of Hernden and his teammates, Green is the founder and president of the Sports Family Club. This organization works to enrich children's lives through positive sports and activities.

Hernden's coaches and teammates supported him however they could. The league's three all-star teams all put yellow stickers with the initials "CH" on the backs of their batting helmets. They printed all-star T-shirts with "CH" in a yellow circle on the sleeve. Sometimes opponents asked what the initials stood for. The players in Hernden's league proudly answered that they were in honor of a teammate's father and his brave struggle.

More than anything, Hernden's coaches tried to make practices focused but light-hearted. "We always tried to keep practice fun," Green said. "Although as coaches we may think it to be serious at times, it's still a game."

One day after practice, Hernden decided he wanted his friends, their parents, and his coaches—his *other* baseball family—to visit his dad. Somehow, all these people squeezed into Charlie's small room. As Hernden sat next to his father, holding his hand, the all-star team sang "Take Me Out to the Ballgame." Most of the adults in the room could barely sing through their tears. The kids carried the tune.

Charlie died only a couple of days later. Hernden's whole team went to the funeral. And the next morning, Hernden was the first one at batting practice. "I gave him a big hug," Coach Green recalled, "and told him how much I admired him." Hernden's teammates dedicated the whole season to Charlie. And it was a good season. The team came very, *very* close to winning the district championship. They lost in the bottom of the last inning by a single run.

Naturally, they were disappointed. But they also understood the big picture. By standing together with a teammate in his darkest days, they had learned something. It was a much more important lesson than how to throw to the cutoff man or stay in front of the ball. They had learned perspective. Soon after their loss, Hernden and his teammates were throwing a ball around and having fun again. They knew that life can be serious, but baseball is a game.

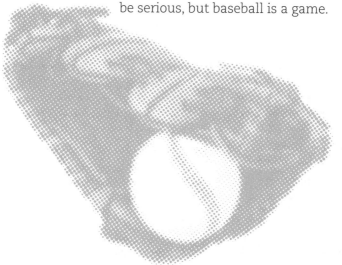

SELECTED BIBLIOGRAPHY

Frost, Mark. *The Greatest Game Ever Played*. New York: Hyperion Books, 2002.

Herzog, Brad. *Francis and Eddie*. Pacific Grove, California: Why Not Books, 2013.

Hillary, Sir Edmund. *High Adventure: The True Story of the First Ascent of Mount Everest*. New York: Oxford University Press, 2003.

Kozlowski, Rick. "I Won It for Carol Anne." *The Journal*. August 1, 2010.

Krentzman, Jackie. "And the Band Played On." *Stanford Magazine*. November/December 2002.

Lake, Thomas. "The Legacy of Wes Leonard." *Sports Illustrated*. February 20, 2012.

Lazdowski, Paul. "Dick and Rick Hoyt Honored with Statue." *The Boston Globe*. April 8, 2013.

Murray, Rheana. "Wheelchair-Bound Football Player Takes the Field and Scores Game's Final Touchdown." *New York Daily News*. November 3, 2011.

Steptoe, Sonja. "The Dogged Pursuit of Excellence." *Sports Illustrated*. February 11, 1991.

Tygiel, Jules. *Baseball's Great Experiment: Jackie Robinson and His Legacy*. New York: Oxford University Press, 1983.

Wallechinksy, David. *The Complete Book of the Olympics*. New York: Penguin Books, 1988.

Winerip, Michael. "Phelps's Mother Recalls Helping Her Son Find Gold-Medal Focus." *The New York Times*. August 8, 2008.

Wolff, Alexander. "The Shot Heard Round the World." *Sports Illustrated*. December 28, 1992.

INDEX

Interior photo credits: Dot pattern images created by Michelle Lee Lagerroos; page 3: based on a photo by © Ron Chapple/Dreamstime.com; page 4: AP Photo/Lisa Poole; page 8: based on a photo by © Nikolay Kuleshin/Dreamstime.com; page 10: AP Photo/Adam Bird; page 14: Bettmann/Corbis / AP Images; page 17: based on a photo by © Zhukovsky/Dreamstime.com; page 20: based on a photo by © Alexander Pladdet/Dreamstime.com; page 23: Copyright Bettmann/Corbis / AP Images; page 26: based on a photo by © Pixattitude/Dreamstime.com; page 28: AP Photo/Mark J. Terrill; page 31: based on a photo by © Hipering/Dreamstime.com; page 32: AP Photo/Julie Oliver, Ottawa Citizen; page 35: based on a photo by © Amy S. Myers/Dreamstime.com; page 40: based on a photo by © Cherezoff/Dreamstime.com; page 41: AP Photo/Ed Betz; page 42: AP Photo/Kevork Djansezian; page 46: AP Photo/Rob Stapleton; page 48: based on a photo by © Milous Chab/Dreamstime.com; page 50: AP Photo/Oakland Tribune/Robert Stinnett; page 57: based on a photo by © Alexander Raths/Dreamstime.com; page 58: AP Photo; page 61: based on a photo by © Galantnie/Dreamstime.com; page 62: based on photos by © Anna Dudko/Dreamstime.com and © Jose Tejo/Dreamstime.com; page 64: based on a photo by © Rmarmion/Dreamstime.com; page 67: Press Association via AP Images; page 68: based on a photo by © Gennaro86/Dreamstime.com; page 71: Press Association via AP Images; page 73: based on a photo by © Alexander Pladdet/Dreamstime.com; page 76: AP Photo/Jim Mone; page 78: based on a photo by © Joseph Helfenberger/Dreamstime.com; page 81: AP Photo/The Free Lance-Star, Peter Cihelka; page 84: based on a photo by © Glenda Powers/Dreamstime.com; page 86: Sam Schulman / Copyright Bettmann/Corbis / AP Images; page 89: based on a photo by © Heysues23/Dreamstime.com; page 95: based on a photo by © Stuart Monk/Dreamstime.com

ABOUT THE AUTHOR

Brad Herzog is the author of more than 30 books for children, including more than two dozen sports books. He has also published three travel memoirs in addition to a fourth book for adults, *The Sports 100*, which ranks and profiles the 100 most important people in U.S. sports history. For his freelance magazine writing (including *Sports Illustrated* and *Sports Illustrated Kids*), Brad has won three gold medals from the Council for Advancement and Support of Education. Brad travels all over the United States visiting schools as a guest author. His website, **bradherzog.com**, includes information about his other books and about his school visits and presentations. Brad lives on California's Monterey Peninsula with his wife and two sons.

Find great sports stories
in all the 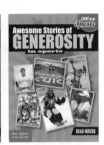 books

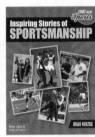

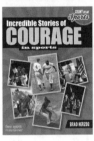

Download a free leader's guide at freespirit.com.

Encourage enthusiasm for reading and inspire positive character development with these powerful stories that highlight character building in sports. Each book features a wide variety of historical and contemporary stories of male and female athletes from around the world. The Count on Me: Sports series demonstrates the power and inspiration of true character. For ages 8–13. *Paperback; 104–112 pp.; 2-color; B&W photos; 5⅛" x 7"*

Interested in purchasing multiple quantities and receiving volume discounts?
Contact edsales@freespirit.com or call 1.800.735.7323 and ask for Education Sales.

Many Free Spirit authors are available for speaking engagements, workshops, and keynotes. Contact speakers@freespirit.com or call 1.800.735.7323.

www.freespirit.com